A GODWARD GAZE

THE HOLY PURSUIT OF JOHN CALVIN

DAVID S. STEELE

ISBN: 978-1095816462

Cover design: Stephen Melniszyn, Stephen Melniszyn Designs

Interior layout: John Manning

To my parents,

Dr. David and Valaura Steele

For nurturing my mind with Christ-centered resolve.
For cultivating a holy dependence upon God's Word.
For always directing my gaze Godward.

TABLE OF CONTENTS

INTRODUCTION

John Bunyan penned the beloved book, *Pilgrim's Progress* in a Bedford prison cell. He was incarcerated from 1660-1672 for violating a law which prohibited religious gatherings outside the framework of the established Church of England.

Pilgrim's Progress is an allegorical tale about Christian, a man who made haste from the City of Destruction. This man was burdened by a load of sin, which was strapped to his back. He not only understood the dilemma of David; he understood the dilemma of every sinner: "For my iniquities have gone over my head; like a heavy burden they are too heavy for me" (Ps. 38:4).

The man in *Pilgrim's Progress* wore a soiled wardrobe, which was soaked in sin (Isa. 64:6). As such, he was spiritually dead (Eph. 2:1; John 5:25). He was spiritually blind and unable to see the light and glory of the gospel (John 3:3; 1 Cor. 2:14). He was spiritually paralyzed; enslaved in sin and unable to come to Christ apart from God's empowerment (John 6:44; 63-65). He was spiritually alienated and separated from God; a stranger to the promises of God. He was spiritually deaf; unable to hear and as a result unable to respond to the call of the Savior (John 8:43-47). He was lost; without hope and without God in the world (Eph. 2:12). He was spiritually destitute. Simply put, he was a spiritual slave; a prisoner enchained by sin's vicious power (John 8:34).

Recognizing his desperate condition, Christian cried out, "What must I do to be saved?" (Acts 2:37-38). A man named Evangelist directs him to the narrow gate (Matt. 7:13) and exhorts him to flee the wrath to come (Matt. 3:7).

Upon hearing the warning of Evangelist, Christian began to run. Bunyan describes the man's urgency in unforgettable words: "Now he had not run far from his own door, when his wife and children (perceiving it) began to cry after him to return but the man put fingers in his ears, and ran on, crying, 'Life! Life! eternal life! So he looked not behind him, but fled toward the middle of the plain."[1] The remainder of the book is the tale of a man on a mission as he makes his way to the Celestial City.

Christian's journey from the City of Destruction to the shores of the Celestial City is a journey that each one of God's elect must travel. The pages of church history reveal a host of men and women who made haste from the City of Destruction and were awakened by the sovereign promptings and power of the Holy Spirit and led them to their heavenly home. *A Godward Gaze* is a snapshot of a man on mission. It is about one man who set his sights on the Celestial City and never looked back. His name is John Calvin.

---

[1] John Bunyan, *The Complete Works of John Bunyan* (Marshallton: The National Foundation for Christian Education, 1968), 12-13.

1
A MAN ON MISSION

John Calvin was a man with holy pursuits. He was a man with a Godward gaze. His pilgrimage began in Noyon, France on July 10, 1509. His mother died when he was only five years of age. In 1521, Calvin enrolled in the *College de Montage* in Paris. Here, he would study logic, rhetoric, and the arts—the very essence of a classical education. Additionally, he would labor over three languages—Latin, Greek, and Hebrew.

The next stop on Calvin's educational pilgrimage was Bourges and Orleans, where he would study law from 1528-1533. However, sometime between 1533-1534, he experienced a "sudden conversion" and fled from Paris to Basel, Switzerland, where he would begin writing the first edition of the *Institutes of the Christian Religion*. As one might expect, Calvin devoured the Bible and pursued the Protestant cause with great passion. Listen to how he expresses his deepest desire and how God turned the key to his heart: "In short, while the one great object was to live in seclusion without being known, God so led me about through different turnings and changes that he never permitted me to rest in any place, until in spite of my natural disposition, he brought me forth to public notice."[2] The turning of this "divine key"

---

[2] John Calvin, Cited in David W. Hall, *The Legacy of John Calvin* (Phillipsburg: Presbyterian & Reformed, 2008), 49.

set Calvin on a Christ-centered trajectory that changed his life personally and professionally, and would soon change the world. Calvin completed the first edition of the *Institutes* in 1536. That same year, he arrived in Geneva and settled in as a pastor. It was the flamboyant William Farel who convinced the French Reformer to stay in Geneva: "William Farel detained him in Geneva, not so much by counsel and exhortation as by dreadful imprecation, which I felt to be as if God had from heaven laid his mighty hand upon me to arrest me."[3] The fiery Farel added, "If you do not assist us in this work of the Lord, the Lord will punish you."[4]

Calvin was exiled to Strasbourg in April of 1538, a providential detour that would last until 1541. He and Farel refused to serve communion to carnal, unrepentant people, which led to their untimely departure. During those years, he worked hard to shepherd Protestant exiles and ministered God's love in practical ways. Calvin's friend, Theodore Beza believed that the exile to Strasbourg was due to divine providence and enabled the young Reformer to grow as a pastor and theologian. As usual, God's providential designs would be for the good of his people and to the praise of his glory (Hab. 2:14).

In 1540, Calvin married the widow Idelette de Bure. The following year, the couple returned to Geneva on September 13th. Calvin made his ascent into the pulpit and began his exposition at the very place he left off when he had been exiled three years earlier. During this time, French Huguenots sought refuge in Geneva under Calvin's leadership in order to escape the brutal reign of Mary Tudor. John

---

3   Ibid, 51.
4   William Farel, Cited Steven J. Lawson, *The Expository Genius of John Calvin* (Orlando: Reformation Trust Publishing, 2007), 11.

Knox, a refugee from Scotland, called Calvin's church in Geneva, "the most perfect school of Christ that was ever in the earth since the days of the apostles."

In 1558, Calvin founded the Academy at Geneva. The next year, he revised and completed the final edition of the *Institutes* which is still in print almost five hundred years later.

On May 27, 1564, Calvin died. At his request, he was buried in a common grave to prevent pilgrimages to his gravesite. The man with a Godward gaze could not stand the thought of people memorializing him.

CALVIN'S PURSUIT

Calvin was a sinner like each of us. He battled the sin of pride and fought temptation like every human being. But his pursuit in life was characterized by God's providential grace which led him from place to place, equipping him for a lifetime of ministry. It was God's providential grace that sustained him during his period of exile and sheltered him through the storms of life. It was God's providential grace that empowered him to write, preach, and shepherd people for the glory of God. It was God's providential grace that brought Calvin "through many dangers, toils, and snares."[5] Indeed, it was God's providential grace that rescued his soul from the torments of hell and seated him in the heavenly places in Christ Jesus (Eph. 2:6). This divine providential grace led Calvin to assume a particular posture which is best articulated in Isaiah 66.

> *Thus says the LORD: 'Heaven is my throne, and the earth is my footstool; what is the house that you would build for me, and what is the place of my rest? All these things my*

---

[5]   John Newton, *Amazing Grace*, 1831.

hand has made, and so all these things came to be, declares
the LORD. But this is the one to whom I will look: he who
is humble and contrite in spirit and trembles at my word'
(Isaiah 66:1–2).

John Calvin's gaze was Godward. He was a pious man, driven by God's majesty and a love for Scripture. His holy pursuit, as we shall see, was to live according to Isaiah's timeless wisdom, "… But this is the one to whom I will look: he who is humble and contrite in spirit and trembles at my word" (Isa. 66:2b). But aspiring to live according to Isaiah 66 and actually carrying it out are two different things. Like you and I, Calvin was a fallen man, a sinner. He battled sin and stared temptation in the face. He went into the "boxing ring" of life each day and fought the world, the flesh, and the devil.

The first sentence in the *Institutes* demonstrates how keenly aware he was of his own finitude and propensity to sin. He writes, "Nearly all the wisdom we possess, that is to say, true and sound wisdom, consists of two parts: the knowledge of God and of ourselves."[6] Calvin understood that apart from grace, sinners would flee from God and forsake his law. Apart from sovereign grace, sinners would utterly repudiate the Word of God and the promises of God. Calvin continues, "Because of the bondage of sin by which the will is held bound, it cannot move toward good, much less apply itself thereto: for a movement of this sort is the beginning of conversion to God, which in Scripture is ascribed entirely to God's grace."[7] The grace that Calvin speaks about, not only delivered him from the bonds of a Roman Catholic

---

6   John Calvin, *Institutes of the Christian Religion* (Philadelphia: Westminster Press), 35.

7   Ibid, 2.3.5.

system of works; it freed him from the penalty of sin and the power of sin. He adds:

> *On the other hand, it may be proper to consider what the remedy is which divine grace provides for the correction and cure of natural corruption ... God, therefore, begins the good work in us by exciting in our hearts a desire, a love, and a study of righteousness, or (to speak correctly) by turning, training, and guiding our hearts unto righteousness; and he completes this good work by confirming us into perseverance.*[8]

While Calvin frequently acknowledged the sin that he was delivered from, he also rejoiced in the Savior who enabled him to live a life to the glory of God. The same regenerating work of the Holy Spirit that transformed his stony heart into a heart of flesh was also responsible for sanctifying Calvin's thoughts, will, desires, and the general course of his life. It was the Spirit of God who prompted saving faith. It was the Spirit of God who prompted obedience. Indeed, it was the Spirit of God who led Calvin down the narrow path (Matt. 7:14), the pathway of the blessed man (Ps. 1:1-3). It was the Spirit of God who prompted his Godly gaze and his holy pursuit. It was the Spirit of God who guided Calvin to the shores of the Celestial City. It was the Spirit of God who transformed John Calvin into a man of humility, a man of contrition, and a man who trembled before the Word of God.

A HUMBLE MAN

A humble man is someone who is lowly in disposition. Here is a man of low position, one who is undistinguished and has a modest opinion of himself. A humble man behaves in an unassuming manner and is devoid of haughtiness.

---

[8]   Ibid., 2.3.6.

C.J. Mahaney writes, "Humility is honestly assessing ourselves in light of God's holiness and our sinfulness."[9] Mahaney's approach to humility finds deep support in the Bible:

Finally, all of you, have unity of mind, sympathy, brotherly love, a tender heart, and a humble mind (1 Pet. 3:8).

Whoever humbles himself like this child is the greatest in the kingdom of heaven (Matt. 18:4).

He has told you, O man, what is good; and what does the Lord require of you but to do justice, and to love kindness, and to walk humbly with your God? (Micah 6:8).

Calvin Was Humble Before His God

He understood his position before a holy God. He was intensely aware that he was a recipient of God's grace (Rom. 3:24), that he had been saved by grace alone, through faith alone, in Christ alone (Eph. 2:8-9). Consequently, he understood that his only boast was the cross-work of Jesus Christ. The apostle Paul echoes this realization in his letter to the Corinthians: "For I decided to know nothing among you except Jesus Christ and him crucified" (1 Cor. 2:2). The boast of the apostle is Calvin's boast as well: "But far be it from me to boast except in the cross of our Lord Jesus Christ, by which the world has been crucified to me, and I to the world" (Gal. 6:14).

Calvin understood the absolute contrast between the sinfulness of man and the majesty of God, what theologians refer to as the Creator-creature distinction. In a typical lucid moment, the French reformer writes, "... Man is never sufficiently touched and affected by the awareness of his lowly

---

9   C.J. Mahaney, *Humility: True Greatness* (Wheaton: Crossway Books, 2005), 22.

state until he has compared himself with God's majesty."[10] Such is the pattern of Calvin's humility. This man was humble before his God.

Calvin Was Humble Before People

Humility is the foundation of Christian character that Calvin modeled so well in his life and ministry. Such a posture, however, was not easy for the zealous reformer. The legalists opposed him and the libertines named their dogs after him. But he remained steadfast. He remained humble despite the hatred which was foisted upon him. His attraction to men who model humility shows the supreme value he placed on this virtue: "A saying of Chrysostom's has always pleased me very much, that the foundation of our philosophy is humility ... So if you ask me concerning the precepts of Christian religion, first, second, third, and always I would answer, 'Humility.'"[11] Calvin himself weighs in on the importance of humility:

Those who have joined together the two things, to think humbly of ourselves before God and yet hold our own righteousness in some estimation, have hitherto taught a pernicious hypocrisy. For if we confess to God contrary to what we feel, we wickedly lie to him; but we cannot feel as we ought without seeing that everything like a ground of boasting is completely crushed.[12]

John Calvin was a consistently humble man who understood the value of a lowly disposition. Surely his life is a worthy model for us to emulate.

---

[10]   *Institutes*, 1.1.3.
[11]   Ibid., 2.2.11.
[12]   *Institutes*, (Peabody: Hendrickson, 2008), 3.12.6.

A Contrite Man

The Old Testament virtue of contrition comes from a Hebrew word that means "stricken, smitten, or crushed in spirit." A person who demonstrates biblical contrition assesses himself in light of Scripture. Such a person has a feeling of intense remorse and bears the weight of guilt for his or her sinful shortcomings.

Yet, the Bible offers hope to the contrite person: "The LORD is near to the brokenhearted and saves the crushed in spirit" (Ps. 34:18). John Calvin, as we shall see, modeled the virtue of contrition.

Calvin Was a Man of Christ-Exalting Contrition

His contrition was Christ-exalting because he willingly acknowledged the One he had offended and that Christ alone could forgive him and free him from his sin. No work could forgive him; no prayer could forgive him; no priest could forgive him.[13]

As beneficiaries of the Protestant Reformation, this is a truth we often take for granted. Even worse, some professing evangelicals have begun to subtly fall under the spell of the Roman Catholic church and either forget free grace or ignore it altogether. Now is the time for a new reformation; a radical rekindling of the precious truths that drove men such as Calvin, Luther, and Knox to their knees in contrition as they celebrated the free grace that was theirs in Christ alone!

---

[13] "Rome required three things in repentance, i.e, compunction of heart, confession of the mouth, and satisfaction of work - they at the same time teach that these are necessary to obtain the pardon of sins." See John Calvin, *Institutes*, 407. Luther shows that "those who set down these three parts of repentance, speak neither according to the Scripture nor the ancient fathers."

A Trembling Man

John Calvin was a man who trembled at God's Word. Recall the great reality of Isaiah 66:2b—"But this is the one to whom I will look: he who is humble and contrite in spirit and trembles at my word." Calvin notes, "Therefore illumined by (the Spirit's) power, we believe neither by our own nor by anyone else's judgment that Scripture is from God; but above human judgment we affirm with utter certainty that it has flowed to us from the very mouth of God by the ministry of men."[14] So the Protestant reformer not only held the Word of God in high esteem; he trembled at God's Word.

Calvin Revered the Truth of God's Word

The Word was preeminent in the mind of the Reformer. Steven Lawson writes:

> *Calvin stood firmly on the chief cornerstone of the Reformation*—sola Scriptura, *or 'Scripture alone.' He believed Scripture was the* verbum Dei—*the Word of God—and it alone should regulate church life, not popes, councils, or traditions.* Sola Scriptura *identified the Bible as the sole authority of God in His church, and Calvin wholeheartedly embraced it, insisting that the Bible was the authoritative, inspired, inerrant, and infallible Word of God.*[15]

The Word of God was the highest authority in Calvin's life. The *sola Scriptura* principle governed his life, fueled his resolved, and kindled his affections.

---

[14]   John Calvin, *Institutes of the Christian Religion* (Philadelphia: Westminster Press), 80.

[15]   Steven J. Lawson, *The Expository Genius of John Calvin*, 25

Calvin Responded to the Truth of God's Word

The preacher from Geneva was a fallen man. But the Holy Spirit quickened his sinful heart. The Holy Spirit regenerated Calvin's recalcitrant heart which enabled him to respond obediently to Scripture and glorify the Lord. To that end, he proclaimed the Word of God faithfully with all the passion he could muster.

Calvin Rejoiced in the Truth of God's Word

He rejoiced in *mysterious* doctrines like the Trinity and the hypostatic union. He rejoiced in *difficult* doctrines like eternal punishment and predestination. And he rejoiced in *paradoxical* doctrines like the sovereignty of God and the responsibility of man and the coupling of evangelism and election. Indeed, this is a man who trembled at God's Word.

WHY DOES JOHN CALVIN MATTER?

Who was this man who had the ability to capture hearts and minds by riveting their attention on the majesty and glory of God? Who was this man who has been caricatured, perhaps more than any man in church history?

John Calvin was a man whose gaze was Godward. His holy pursuit was rare among men and a model to followers of Christ. But why does this man who lived over five hundred years ago matter? What lessons can he teach us?

1. Calvin understood that people are transformed by truth.

We live in an age in which technique is king and pragmatism is queen. The church has fallen prey to this vicious cycle. We tend to do what works and only invest in the kinds of things that promise immediate results. Steven Lawson adds, "The church is always looking for better methods in order to reach the world. But God is looking for better men who will devote themselves to his biblically mandated method for advancing his kingdom, namely, preaching—and not just any kind of preaching, but expository preaching."[16] So Calvin expended a great deal of energy in crafting expository sermons and preaching in the power of the Spirit. In a day when preaching is being marginalized and theology is being ignored, we need to remember what Calvin understood, namely, people are transformed by truth.

2. *Calvin understood and modeled the need for courage in times of adversity and persecution.*

Calvin lived in a time when Protestants were burned at the stake because they were being transformed by the truth. His courage and tenacity inspired other men and women of God to stand their ground for the sake of biblical principles. This man was committed to boldly proclaiming the truth no matter the cost.

3. *Calvin reminds us of the sinfulness of the human heart and the desperate need for God's grace.*

The flaws in Calvin himself remind us of the sinfulness of sin. He was deeply aware of the sin in his own life. But he was also aware of the transforming reality of grace. His life is a testimony to this great truth. Calvin was *simul justus et peccator*—simultaneously righteous and sinful.

---

[16]   Ibid, 18-19.

4. *Calvin reminds us what one man with a Godward gaze can accomplish in Christ's strength.*

Wayne Pickens argues, "God uses people to reach people."[17] Calvin walked by the power of the Holy Spirit (Gal. 5:16) and lived a crucified life (Gal. 2:20). Any good fruit that he bore was attributed to the mighty work of God.

5. *Calvin reminds us of the sufficiency of Christ and his work on the cross for sinners.*

The cry of Calvin's heart was nothing less than the Lord Jesus Christ. He constantly and consistently pointed sinners to Christ and his cross. Both pulpit and pen served Christ uniquely in his generation. His faithfulness continues to bear much fruit in our generation.

John Calvin was a man on mission. The Godward gaze was a defining mark of his life. He was a man of humility. He was a man of contrition. He was a man who trembled at God's Word. May the French Reformer's life serve as an inspiration for each of us to live the Christian life with vibrancy to the glory of God. May we serve God in the "theater of his glory" as Calvin liked to call it. May his courage embolden us in the difficult days ahead. When the days grow dark, when persecutions escalate, and when our freedom begins to erode, may we remember the motto which is etched in the Genevan stone, *post tenebras lux*, "after darkness light." May his humility, contrition, and trembling before the Word of God mark our lives as well. And may the contemporary pulpit be a reflection of Calvin's pulpit; may men of God stand in the pulpit and deliver God's Word so the saints might be strengthened, edified, convicted, challenged, encouraged, and equipped!

---

[17]   Wayne C. Pickens, *Pleasing God or Man?*, June 2009.

Calvin writes, "Let them edify the body of Christ. Let them devastate Satan's reign. Let them pasture the sheep, kill the wolves, instruct and exhort the rebellious. Let them bind and loose, thunder and lightning, if necessary, but let them do all according to the Word of God."[18] May the unwavering Godward gaze of Calvin point you toward the Savior, the Lord Jesus Christ—the uncreated One who is Lord over all things. May Calvin's holy pursuit of the living God inspire and embolden you. And may his steadfast devotion to God, his unswerving allegiance to truth, and his resolve to faithfully finish the race encourage you—all the way to the Celestial City!

The remainder of this study will excavate the deep doctrinal truths of Isaiah 66:2 and reveal how we, along with Calvin must cast our eyes Godward. This critical verse will ignite our affections and inform our holy pursuits. If we are to be a people whose gaze is directed Godward, we must be humble, be contrite in spirit, and tremble before God's Word.

---

[18]   Cited in Steven J. Lawson, *The Expository Genius of John Calvin*, 29.

2
A MAN OF HUMILITY

John Calvin was a man of deep humility. While he has been caricatured as mean-spirited, bigoted, and narrow-minded, nothing could be further from the truth. "He was a man of deep and lasting affection, passionately concerned for the cause of Christ in the world; a man who burned himself out for the gospel."[19] Even in the days after he was exiled from Geneva, he refused to grow bitter. He resisted the urge to feel sorry for himself. He rejected the urge to retaliate. Rather, he pursued a posture of humility. He encouraged his friend, William Farel, to tread upon this God-centered path: "Let us humble ourselves, therefore, unless we wish to strive with God when He would humble us."[20] Calvin not only commended this path to others; he was constrained to walk this path himself. By God's grace, he maintained the posture of humility for the remainder of his earthly days.

THE POSTURE OF HUMILITY

Humility may be one of the most misunderstood virtues in Scripture. But understanding humility is the first essential step in becoming a person whose gaze is Godward. Humility is "honestly assessing ourselves in light of God's holiness and our sinfulness."[21] The Old Testament word for humility

---

19   *Letters of John Calvin* (Edinburgh: The Banner of Truth Trust, 2018), xiii.
20   Ibid, 25.
21   C.J. Mahaney, *Humility: True Greatness* (Wheaton: Crossway Books, 2005), 22.

means "to be gentle; i.e. pertaining to being unpretentious and straightforward, suggesting a lack of arrogance, hubris, or pride."[22] Joel R. Beeke and Paul M. Smalley observe, "Humility and brokenness over sin are fitting responses to the Word, because when we hear the Word, we are in the presence of the infinite and holy Creator of heaven and earth. We do not stand in judgment over the Bible; rather, in the Bible, God stands in judgment over us, to bless or to curse, to save or condemn."[23] Several passages in the Old Testament help clarify the meaning of this important concept:

Toward the scorners he is scornful, but to the humble he gives favor (Prov. 3:34).

Rejoice greatly, O daughter of Zion! Shout aloud, O daughter of Jerusalem! Behold, your king is coming to you; righteous and having salvation is he, humble and mounted on a donkey, on a colt, the foal of a donkey (Zech. 9:9).

You save a humble people, but your eyes are on the haughty to bring them down (2 Sam. 22:28).

The New Testament word for humility describes a person who is unpretentious and lowly; one who is humble in status. A humble person is meek and mild. The German philosopher, Friedrich Nietzsche claimed that "meekness is weakness" and "might is right." Jesus disagrees. He says, "Blessed are the meek, for they shall inherit the earth" (Matt. 5:5). The word "meek" was originally used to describe a stallion that was being reigned in. The word describes a horse being controlled by a bit and bridle. The portrait of meekness is this: *strength under control*. Calvin describes the mindset of a man committed to humility:

---

22   Swanson, J. (1997). *Dictionary of Biblical Languages with Semantic Domains (Old Testament)*. Oak Harbor: Logos Research Systems, Inc.

23   Joel R. Beeke and Paul M. Smalley, *Reformed Systematic Theology: Revelation and God - Volume 1* (Wheaton: Crossway, 2019), 342.

For the pious mind realizes that the punishment of the impious and wicked and the reward of life eternal for the righteous equally pertain to God's glory. Besides, this mind restrains itself from sinning, not out of dread of punishment alone; but, because it loves and reveres God as Father, it worships and adores him as Lord. Even if there were no hell, it would still shudder at offending him alone.[24]

Scripture reveals the posture for biblical humility: "But he gives more grace. Therefore it says, 'God opposes the proud, but gives grace to the humble.' Submit yourselves therefore to God. Resist the devil, and he will flee from you" (Jas. 4:6-7).

A Humble Person Submits to God

The Greek term translated *submit* is derived from a military term which means "to obey; to be subordinate; to render obedience." The humble person, therefore, joyfully submits to God's sovereign designs. This person is eager to listen to God, learn from him, and obey the Word of God.

A Humble Person Resists the Devil

Resist is a word of hostility, which means "to oppose or take a stand against." We resist the devil when he accuses us. We resist him when he tempts us to sin. We resist the devil when we remove ungodly temptations from our lives. One way to resist the devil is to stand firm:

- Noah stood firm despite the mocking crowd that surrounded him.
- Moses stood firm despite the diabolical schemes of Pharaoh.
- Joseph stood firm despite the rebels who surrounded him.

---

[24] *Institutes*, 1.3.2.

- Nehemiah stood firm despite the nitpicking crowd who mocked and belittled him.
- Job stood firm despite a wife who pleaded with him to 'curse God and die.'
- Samuel stood firm despite a nation who compromised and a king who capitulated.
- Josiah stood firm despite the compromise perpetuated by the culture and other ungodly kings.
- Isaiah stood firm despite the military invasion of the enemies of God.
- Jeremiah and Ezekiel stood firm despite the rampant idolatry that surrounded them.
- Daniel stood firm despite an empire who opposed the plans and purposes of a holy God.
- Amos stood firm despite the corruption and apostasy that plagued his culture.
- Micah stood firm despite the crooked men who oppressed the poor.
- John the Baptist stood firm and endured a horrible death to the glory of God.
- The apostle Paul stood firm despite the weaknesses, insults, hardships, persecutions, and calamities.
- Jesus Christ stood firm despite being tempted in all ways.

God's Word is clear about our responsibility to stand firm:

Be watchful, stand firm in the faith, act like men, be strong (1 Cor. 16:13).

So then, brothers, stand firm and hold to the traditions that you were taught by us, either by our spoken word or by our letter (2 Thess. 2:15).

By Silvanus, a faithful brother as I regard him, I have written briefly to you, exhorting and declaring that this is the true grace of God. Stand firm in it (1 Pet. 5:12).

For freedom Christ has set us free; stand firm therefore, and do not submit again to a yoke of slavery (Gal. 5:1).

"Therefore take up the whole armor of God, that you may be able to withstand in the evil day, and having done all, to stand firm" (Eph. 6:13).

Therefore, my brothers, whom I love and long for, my joy and crown, stand firm thus in the Lord, my beloved (Phil. 4:1).

When we resist the devil, James 4:7 tells us that "he will flee." So a humble person submits to God and resists the devil. Both verbs are written in the aorist tense which suggests that we must make a point-in-time decision to *submit* to God and *resist* the devil. This is not a hit-and-miss proposition. This is a proactive decision. This is the posture of humility.

THE PAYOFF OF HUMILITY

The apostle Paul models this kind of God-centered humility (2 Cor. 12:8-10) as he faced persecution, hardship, and calamity. His life is a testimony of how God uses humility in the lives of his people. Notice a few benefits of humility.

God is Drawn to the Humble

C.J. Mahaney remarks, "Humility draws the gaze of our sovereign God."[25] The face of God is attracted to the person who is committed to maintaining a posture of humility. The humble person draws the attention of a holy God.

God Hears the Humble

2 Chronicles 7:14 says, "If my people who are called by my name humble themselves, and pray and seek my face and turn from their wicked ways, then I will hear from heaven and

---

[25]   C.J. Mahaney, *Humility: True Greatness* , 19.

will forgive their sin and heal their land." In 2 Chronicles 34:26-27, we see how God listens to the heart of the humble:

> *But to the king of Judah, who sent you to inquire of the LORD, thus shall you say to him, Thus says the LORD, the God of Israel: Regarding the words that you have heard, because your heart was tender and you humbled yourself before God when you heard his words against this place and its inhabitants, and you have humbled yourself before me and have torn your clothes and wept before me, I also have heard you, declares the LORD.*

Clearly, when our hearts are humble and tender before God, he demonstrates an eagerness to listen to us.

God Exalts the Humble

"For though the LORD is on high, he regards the lowly, but the haughty he knows from afar" (Ps. 138:6). While conventional wisdom suggests that "pride pays," and postmodern prophets urge us to "look out for number one," the Word of God paints an entirely different portrait. James 4:10 says, "Humble yourselves before the Lord, and he will exalt you." The psalmist adds, "The LORD lifts up the humble, he casts the wicked to the ground" (Ps. 147:6). Peter confirms this mighty reality: "Humble yourselves, therefore, under the mighty hand of God so that at the proper time he may exalt you" (1 Pet. 5:6).

God Empowers the Humble

The apostle Paul learned this lesson firsthand. After begging God to remove his thorn in the flesh, the Lord responds decisively: "My grace is sufficient for you, for my power is made perfect in weakness" (2 Cor. 2:9a). Notice Paul's reaction: "Therefore I will boast all the more gladly of my weaknesses, so that the power of Christ may rest upon me. For the sake of Christ, then, I am content with weaknesses, insults, hardships, persecutions, and calamities. For when I am weak then I am strong" (2 Cor. 2:9b-10). Paul learned the supreme benefit of humility and experienced God's empowering presence as a result. Kris Lundgaard remarks, "God's radiating majesty kills the rotten marrow of sin and replaces it with humility. A heart humbled by God's terrible majesty can begin its recovery and grow strong. Sin can't thrive in a humble heart."[26] In counterintuitive fashion, then, the humble person is empowered by God.

Humility Corrects the Vision of the Humble

While pride immobilizes its victims and renders them ineffective, humility has the opposite effect. Humility restores our vision and enables us to not only grasp the grandeur of God; it also enables us to gaze at the glory of God. Stephen Nichols adds, "Humility enables us to see the glory of God, and seeing the glory of God takes us to deeper levels of humility, which enables fuller and deeper glimpses of God's glory."[27] Humility, then, propels us forward by the grace of God and for the glory of God.

THE PRINCIPLES OF HUMILITY

John Calvin consistently modeled a life of humility. David W. Hall explains the essence of Calvin's theological method. He writes, "Humility is characteristic of this great system of thought, and it was exemplified in the life of Calvin."[28] Four principles help undergird a person who is committed to pursuing humility.

---

[26] Kris Lundgaard, *The Enemy Within: Straight Talk About the Power and Defeat of Sin* (Philipsburg: Presbyterian & Reformed, 1998), 128.

[27] Stephen J. Nichols, *Heaven on Earth: Capturing Jonathan Edwards's Vision of Living in Between* (Wheaton: Crossway Books, 2006), 98

[28] David W. Hall, *The Legacy of John Calvin: His Influence on the Modern World* (Phillipsburg: Presbyterian & Reformed, 2008), 79.

By Understanding Who I Am

Calvin understood this important aspect of humility. We have seen how this principle is at the core of Calvin's theological framework: "Our wisdom, insofar as it ought to be deemed true and solid wisdom, consists almost entirely of two parts: the knowledge of God and of ourselves."[29] This principle helps launch Calvin's Institutes into the theological stratosphere! So a person who is pursuing humility is careful to understand who he is and how the Scripture views him.

By Understanding Who God Is

It is the commitment to knowing God and knowing ourselves that leads to wisdom which is informed by humility. Again, Calvin is on target: "… We cannot seriously aspire to him before we begin to become displeased with ourselves … Accordingly, the knowledge of ourselves not only arouses us to seek God, but also, as it were, leads us by the hand to find him."[30] The humble person pursues God daily in his Word and communes with him in prayer.

By Embracing the Doctrines of Grace

When we believe what the Bible says about our fallen condition, when we truly embrace it—we will be humbled (Rom. 3:10-18; John 8:34: Eph. 1:1-2). When we believe what the Bible says about our salvation, namely, that it is grounded in eternity past by a sovereign God who chose us unconditionally - we will be humbled (Eph. 1:3-11; 2 Tim. 1:9). When we believe what the Bible says about the ministry of the Holy Spirit and his ministry of drawing us to the Son—we will be humbled (John 6:44, 65). When we believe what the Bible says about a God who promises to preserve our salva-

---

[29]   *Institutes*, 1.2.2.
[30]   Ibid, 1.1.2.

tion until the last day—we will be humbled (Phil. 1:6; John 10:28-29; Jude 24-25). Spurgeon skillfully summarizes the doctrines of grace for us:

> *I have my own private opinion that there is no such thing as preaching Christ and him crucified, unless we preach what nowadays is called Calvinism. It is a nickname to call it Calvinism; Calvinism is the gospel, and nothing else. I do not believe we can preach the gospel, if we do not preach justification by faith, without works; nor unless we preach the sovereignty of God in his dispensation of grace; nor unless we exalt the electing, unchangeable, eternal, immutable, conquering love of Jehovah; nor do I think we can preach the gospel, unless we base it upon the special and particular redemption of his elect and chosen people which Christ wrought out upon the cross; nor can I comprehend a gospel which lets saints fall away after they are called, and suffers the children of God to be burned in the fires of damnation after having once believed in Jesus.*[31]

The Calvinism that Spurgeon describes is humble by definition. The very notion of receiving sovereign grace humbles every sinner who receives it! "Humble Calvinism" is the theme of J.A. Medders' excellent book. Pastor Medders urges readers, "Live with a holy happiness in God's sovereign and sustaining grace. Spread the word about the God who is rich in mercy, slow to anger, and abounding in faithful love. And for those of us who are happy to be called Calvinists, from now on let's make sure we are humble and happy Calvinists."[32] When we embrace this gospel—we will be humbled.

---

[31] See C.H. Spurgeon, *A Defense of Calvinism*, quoted by J.I. Packer in his "Introductory Essay" to John Owen, *The Death of Death in the Death of Christ* (London: Banner of Truth, 1959), 10.

[32] J.A. Medders, *Humble Calvinism* (Purcellville: The Good Book Company, 2019), loc. 1697.

By Measuring Everything Through the Cross of Christ

When every plan, intention, dream, and activity is measured through the cross, we purposefully pursue humility. Pastors, then, should preach every sermon with the cross in view. Every class and every counseling session should place the cross of Christ at the center. "The cross convinces us to make Christ's substitutionary atonement our only boast," writes William Farley.[33] "In other words, because of the cross, we can boast in God's love despite the complete absence of personal merit. We deserve damnation."[34]

When we measure everything through the cross, our perspective is renewed and our purpose is clarified. John Piper adds, "The cross is the place our sin is seen as most horrible and where God's free grace shines most brightly."[35] Apart from the cross of Christ, our judgment is sealed and we are doomed; we stand condemned for all eternity under 10,000 degrees of white-hot fury. Such a truth is guaranteed to humble us!

The gospel, then, propels us on the path of humility. Indeed, apart from the gospel, we will always gravitate to pride (Ps. 138:6; 1 Pet. 5:5; Jas. 4:6). So, we pursue humility by preaching the gospel to ourselves each day. We remind ourselves that apart from grace, we would spend eternity in hell. Apart from grace, we would bear the weight of all our sin and stand condemned. May the covenant-keeping God grant grace to each of us as we walk with his Son in humility.

---

[33] William Farley, *Gospel-Powered Humility* (Philipsburg: Presbyterian and Reformed, 2011), Loc. 699.

[34] Ibid.

[35] John Piper, *Seeing Beauty and Saying Beautifully* (Wheaton: Crossway Books, 2014), 24.

3
A MAN OF CONTRITION

People whose gaze is set on the living God not only pursue humility; they are contrite. Recall Isaiah 66:2 - "But this is the one to whom I will look: he who is humble and contrite in spirit and trembles at my word" (Isa. 66:2b). The progression here, I believe, is critical. Notice that humility precedes contrition. Humility is the trigger, if you will, for contrition. Humility is the necessary prerequisite for anyone to stand among the contrite.

THE POSTURE OF CONTRITION

The Old Testament word for *contrite* comes from a word that means "lame or crippled." The term applies to a person who has been beaten down or broken. *Contrite* describes a person who is penitent; a person who is repentant for being a willing party to sin. Additionally, the Old Testament word for *repentance* means "to turn back; turn around; recover; restore; or to return home." Ezekiel 14:6 says, "Therefore say to the house of Israel, Thus says the Lord God: Repent and turn away from your idols, and turn away your faces from all your abominations." Ezekiel 18:30 says, "Therefore I will judge you, O house of Israel, every one according to his ways, declares the Lord God. Repent and turn from all your transgressions, lest iniquity be your ruin."

The New Testament term for repentance is *metanoia*, which describes a "change of lifestyle; a complete change of mind about sin and righteousness." Theologically, it involves regret or sorrow, accompanied by a true change of heart toward God.[36] The Bible rehearses this theme over and over:

Now after John was arrested, Jesus came into Galilee, proclaiming the gospel of God, and saying, 'The time is fulfilled, and the kingdom of God is at hand; repent and believe in the gospel' (Mark 1:14-15).

The times of ignorance God overlooked, but now he commands all people everywhere to repent … (Acts 17:30).

Repent, therefore, of this wickedness of yours, and pray to the Lord that, if possible, the intent of your heart may be forgiven you (Acts 8:22).

Finally, Paul the apostle links humility with repentance in his address to the Ephesian elders:

And when they came to him, he said to them: "You yourselves know how I lived among you the whole time from the first day that I set foot in Asia, serving the Lord with all humility and with tears and with trials that happened to me through the plots of the Jews; how I did not shrink from declaring to you anything that was profitable, and teaching you in public and from house to house, testifying both to Jews and to Greeks of repentance toward God and of faith in our Lord Jesus Christ (Acts 20:18–21).

The theme of contrition is a high point in the writings of many godly men and deserves our careful attention:

---

[36]   Zodhiates, S. (2000), *The Complete Word Study Dictionary: New Testament*. Chattanooga, TN: AMG Publishers.

Repentance is a supernatural and inward revelation from God, giving a deep consciousness of what I am in His sight, which causes me to loathe and condemn myself, resulting in a bitter sorrow for sin, a holy horror and hatred for sin, a suturing away from or forsaking of sin.[37]

Repentance is a grace of God's Spirit whereby a sinner is inwardly humbled and visibly reformed.[38]

Godly sorrow, however, is chiefly for the trespass against God, so that even if there were no conscience to smite, no devil to accuse, no hell to punish, yet the soul would still be grieved because of the prejudice done to God.[39]

Repentance is a turning from darkness to light. It affects the sinner's whole heart and life. It changes the heart from the power of sin unto God. Every sin strikes at the honor of God, the being of God, the glory of God, the heart of Christ, the joy of the Spirit, and the peace of man's conscience. A truly penitent soul strikes at all sin, hates all, and will labor to crucify all ... Repentance breaks the heart with sighs, sobs, and groans, in that a loving God and Father is offended by sin, a blessed Savior is crucified afresh, and the sweet Comforter, the Spirit, is grieved and vexed. O that you were wise to break off your sins by timely repentance.[40]

People who assume the posture of contrition pay careful attention to biblical mandates and heed the imperatives set forth in Scripture:

Draw near to God, and he will draw near to you. Cleanse your hands, you sinners, and purify your hearts, you dou-

---

[37]   A.W. Pink, *Repentance: What Saith the Scriptures?* Loc. 287-297.

[38]   Thomas Watson, *The Doctrine of Repentance* (Carlisle: Banner of Truth, 1668), 18.

[39]   Ibid, 22.

[40]   Thomas Brooks, Cited in Richard Rushing, Ed. *Voices From the Past* (Carlisle: Banner of Truth, 2009), 286.

ble-minded. Be wretched and mourn and weep. Let your laughter be turned to mourning and your joy to gloom. Humble yourselves before the Lord, and he will exalt you (James 4:8–10).

Draw Near to God

This imperative demands that sinners come close to God with a proper attitude. Such an attitude manifests itself when we submit ourselves to God and resist the devil. Therefore, we assume an attitude of biblical submission. By doing so, we bring a few presuppositions to the table. We confess:

- "God, you are the Creator. I am the creature."

- "God, you call the shots. I obey your Word."

- "God, I am your servant. I am your slave."

When Isaiah drew near to God, he did not come pretentiously; nor did he come with an agenda: "Woe is me! For I am lost; for I am a man of unclean lips, and I dwell in the midst of a people of unclean lips; for my eyes have seen the King, the Lord of hosts" (Isa. 6:5). Likewise, when we draw near to God, we come on *his* terms. We submit to *his* agenda and we surrender every shred of pretense. We do things *his* way. We aim for *his* glory.

Cleanse Our Hands

Cleansing our hands means "to purify or heal." When we draw near to God, we come with an expectation that he will perform a good work of grace in our lives. K.A. Richardson adds, "Cleansing the hands and purifying the heart both recall first the ritual purity required of worshippers and of priests at the temple and second the prophetic call to the purification of the heart."[41] Warren Wiersbe notes, "God gra-

---

41   Richardson. (1997). *James* (Vol. 36, p. 186). Nashville: Broadman & Holman Publishers.

ciously draws near to us when we deal with the sin in our lives that keeps Him at a distance."[42] The very idea of cleansing our hands acknowledges our sinful condition and propensity to be double-minded.

Purify Our Hearts

1 Peter 1:22 says, "Having purified your souls by your obedience to the truth for a sincere brotherly love, love one another earnestly from a pure heart." The need for cleansing and purification is clear since James refers to readers as *sinners* who are *double-minded*.

Bear the Marks of Authentic Contrition

James tells us that the one who bears the marks of authentic contrition is "wretched," which manifests an attitude of lament. This person is in a position of "mourning," which means to grieve over something; in this case—sin. "Laughter has turned to mourning." Finally, this person's joy has "turned to gloom." Why would James call anyone to engage in this kind of activity? The context reveals that he is directing his thoughts to the proud person. This is exactly what such a person needs. This individual needs to have an attitude of grieving or lament. This individual needs to be mourning and weeping. His or her laughter must turn to mourning. His or her joy must turn to gloom! Anyone who offers excuses or shifts blame when confronted for sin is not in a posture of contrition. This train of thought should automatically direct our attention back to James 4:6, where we are confronted with the reality that "God opposes the proud but gives grace to the humble."

Ultimately, assuming the posture of contrition will bear the fragrant fruits of humility. Therefore, we cling to the

---

42   Weirsbe, WW. (1996). *The Bible Exposition Commentary* (Vol. 2, p. 370). Wheaton, IL: Victor Books.

promises of the gospel! Indeed, we recognize that apart from grace, we will never find ourselves in a posture of contrition.

THE PROTOTYPE OF CONTRITION

Job is a fitting example of a man who assumed a posture of contrition. But it took a series of traumatic events to produce a heart that was contrite in spirit.

It all began in Job chapter one when Satan asks for God's permission to afflict Job, a God-fearing man (Job 1:6-8). After God grants this request, Satan strips Job of everything he has, including his ranch, his possessions, and all his children. The only one left standing was Job's wife. Job responds with reverent worship: "Naked I came from my mother's womb, and naked shall I return. The LORD gave, and the LORD has taken away; blessed be the name of the LORD" (Job 1:21). The next verse is revealing: "In all this Job did not sin or charge God with wrong."

The scene shifts in chapter two as Satan approaches God again. Predictably, Job's integrity is reaffirmed: "And the LORD said to Satan, "Have you considered my servant Job, that there is none like him on the earth, a blameless and upright man, who fears God and turns away from evil? He still holds fast his integrity, although you incited me against him to destroy him without reason" (Job 2:3). After Satan assaults Job's character (vv. 5-6), God once again grants Satan permission to afflict Job. Yet this time, the sphere narrows: "And the LORD said to Satan, 'Behold, he is in your hand; only spare his life'" (v. 6).

Satan strikes Job with sores from the soles of his feet to the crown of his head. We find Job seated in the ashes as he scrapes his scabs with a piece of broken pottery (Job 2:7-8). Job initially responds with God-centered faith. When his wife responds with sinful bitterness, Job remains steadfast: "But he said to her, 'You speak as one of the foolish women would speak. Shall we receive good from God, and shall we not receive evil?' In all this Job did not sin with his lips" (Job 2:10).

But fast-forward in the narrative and we find a shift in Job's attitude. He begins by subtlety questioning the purposes of God: "Today also my complaint is bitter; my hand is heavy on account of my groaning. Oh, that I knew where I might find him, that I might come even to his seat! I would lay my case before him and fill my mouth with arguments" (Job 23:2–4). Additionally, he utters a plea that reflects the inner condition of his heart: "If only I had someone who would listen to me and try to see my side! Look, I will sign my name to my defense. Let the Almighty show me that I am wrong. Let my accuser write out the charges against me" (Job 31:35, NLT).

God responds directly and decisively to Job's complaints: "Then the LORD answered Job out of the whirlwind and said: "Who is this that darkens counsel by words without knowledge? Dress for action like a man; I will question you, and you make it known to me" (Job 38:1–3). In this unforgettable exchange, God reminds Job that he is the Creator (Job 38:4-11). He is the Sustainer of the universe (Job 38:12-15). God controls the elements of the universe including the oceans, light, darkness, snow, rain, and thunder (Job 38:16-30). God controls the universe, including the orbits of the planets and stars (Job 38:31-38). He controls the animal kingdom (Job 38:39-41). And God demonstrates sovereign control over all creatures (Job 39:1-30).

God asks Job a pivotal question: "Shall a faultfinder contend with the Almighty? He who argues with God, let him answer it?" (Job 42:2). Job's response is not only revealing; it demonstrates a softened heart which is contrite: "Then Job answered the LORD and said: "Behold, I am of small account; what shall I answer you? I lay my hand on my mouth. I have spoken once, and I will not answer; twice, but I will proceed no further" (Job 40:3–5).

Job acknowledges that he is not the "final criterion of truth."[43] His response to God is an act of worship. And his contrition is laced with reverence and repentance.

> *Then Job answered the LORD and said: 'I know that you can do all things, and that no purpose of yours can be thwarted. 'Who is this that hides counsel without knowledge?' Therefore I have uttered what I did not understand, things too wonderful for me, which I did not know. 'Hear, and I will speak; I will question you, and you make it known to me.' I had heard of you by the hearing of the ear, but now my eye sees you; therefore I despise myself, and repent in dust and ashes" (Job 42:1–6).*

Job's contrite response acknowledges God's omnipotence. He admits that God's purposes can never be thwarted. John Piper asserts:

> *If none of his purposes can be frustrated, then he must be the happiest of all beings … Just as our joy is based on the promise that God is strong enough and wise enough to make all things work together for good, so God's joy is based on that same sovereign control: He makes all things work together for his glory.*[44]

In his previous questioning, Job tried to articulate the mysteries of God's purposes—things too wonderful, which

---

[43]   See John Frame, *Christianity Considered: A Guide for Skeptics and Seekers* (Bellingham: Lexham Press, 2018), Loc. 325.

[44]   John Piper, *Desiring God* (Sisters: Multnomah Books, 1996), 35.

he did not know. So Job admits the foolishness of speaking presumptuously.

In the final analysis, Job's response is repentant: "Therefore I despise myself, and repent in dust and ashes" (Job 42:6). Notice how reverence and repentance are integrally linked. It is significant that Job says, "Therefore." He is saying, "There was a time when I questioned your character. There was a time when I questioned your purposes. There was a time when I questioned your plan. I was dreadfully wrong. My attitude was sinful. Please forgive me!" Job is a prototype of biblical contrition. His godly example is one we should return to again and again.

THE PAYOFF OF CONTRITION

Several practical benefits mark the person who is truly contrite.

God is Drawn to the Heart of the Contrite

Once again, "But this is the one to whom I will look: he who is humble and contrite in spirit and trembles at my word" (Isa. 66:2b). God is favorably disposed to the contrite person. The psalmist writes, "The sacrifices of God are a broken spirit; a broken and contrite heart, O God, you will not despise" (Ps 51:17). Much to the chagrin of the typical Western mindset, God is not drawn to the person who possesses special abilities or has a charismatic personality. God is drawn to the heart of the contrite.

God Revives the Heart of the Contrite

God is not only drawn to the contrite person; he is *with* such a person. Psalm 34:18 says, "The Lord is near to the broken-hearted and saves the crushed in spirit." Scripture tells us that God is transcendent. That is, he is over and above the scope of the universe. His sovereignty is unmatched and unrivaled. Isaiah 57:15a shouts the reality of God's transcendence: "For thus says the One who is high and lifted up, who inhabits eternity, whose name is Holy." God is not only transcendent; he is immanent. That is, he is present with his people as a shepherd tends his sheep: "I dwell in the high and holy place, and also with him who is of a contrite and lowly spirit, to revive the spirit of the lowly, and to revive the heart of the contrite" (Isa. 57:15b).

God Exalts the Person Who Comes Before Him in Humility and Contrition

God opposes the proud man but gives much grace to the humble. Such a person rests confidently in the peace that God provides and walks on a secure path, which is undergirded by a gracious and merciful God (Rom. 15:13).

THE PRINCIPLES OF CONTRITION

Several guiding principles will serve as guardrails, directing the people of God whose gaze is Godward.

Admit the Depth of Sin

Walking the path of contrition involves wrestling with sin and admitting its horrifying depth and foolishness. J.C. Ryle recognizes, "True repentance begins with a knowledge of sin … His pride breaks down. His high thoughts melt away. He sees that he is a great sinner. This is the first step in true repentance."[45] Acknowledging the seriousness of sin is a critical first step for anyone who is seeking to walk contritely before God.

Acknowledge the Horror of Sin

Calvin is an example of a man who acknowledged the depth of his sin. But he went even further. Calvin acknowledged the

---

[45]   J.C. Ryle, *Repentance* (Titus Books, 2012), Loc. 39ff.

horror of sin. "Besides, it is not the mere fear of punishment that restrains him from sin. Loving and revering God as his Father, honoring and obeying him as his Master, although there were no hell, he would revolt at the very idea of offending him.[46] Calvin's contrition was directly related to his hatred of sin.

Realize That Sin Goes Deeper Than You Can Ever Imagine

Probing the depth of our sin is like peeling the layers of an onion. The process is time-consuming and painful. But peeling back layer upon layer of sin is a necessary prerequisite of biblical contrition. Over twenty-five years of pastoral ministry has taught me that probing people with questions is an important part of a biblical counseling strategy. Asking thoughtful and penetrating questions help people go deeper and discover their idolatrous motivations and desires. Once these motivations are identified and exposed, they can be repented of, which is a critical part of the healing process.

Calvin understood the depth and gravity of his sin. He confessed, " … Man is never sufficiently touched and affected by the awareness of his lowly state until he has compared himself with God's majesty."[47] Along with Calvin, we must realize that sin goes deeper than we can ever imagine.

Grieve Over Sin

Authentic contrition involves more than merely being sorry for our sin. Calvin adds:

> *But if forgiveness of sins depends on the conditions to which they bind it, nothing can be more wretched and deplorable than our situation. Contrition they represent as the first step in obtaining pardon; and they exact it as due, that is, full and*

---

[46] *Institutes*, 1.2.2.

[47] Ibid., 1.2.3.

> *complete: meanwhile, they decide not when one may feel se-
> cure having performed this contrition in due measure.*[48]

True repentance should express sorrow over sin. While sorrow may appear like a pointless lament, Scripture is clear about the advantages of this level of grieving: "Sorrow is better than laughter, for by sadness of face the heart is made glad" (Eccles. 7:3). A truly contrite person, will, therefore, grieve over sin.

Confess Sin to God

God is omniscient. He has comprehensive knowledge about all things—past, present, and future. God knows all about our sin. He knows about every sin we have ever committed. He knows about every sin we have yet to commit. He knows when we are tempted to sin. He knows when we yield to sin. He knows when we cherish sin in our hearts. He knows when we hide our sin. Therefore, we must confess our sin to God. The apostle John writes, "If we confess our sins, he is faithful and just to forgive us our sins and to cleanse us from all unrighteousness (1 John 1:9). The apostle establishes his creed in 1 John 1. He essentially says this: "I will walk in the light as he is in the light, confessing my sin daily and resting in my Savior who forgives all my sins." Notice that he affirms the character of God. He admits he is a sinner. He admits that he sins. He confesses his sins. John Newton understood this creed when he uttered those now famous words shortly before his death, "I am a great sinner. And Christ is a great Savior!"[49]

Flee from Sin

One of the telltale signs of a contrite heart is a willingness, ability, and passion to flee from sin. Joseph models this kind

---

[48]   Ibid., 3.4.2.

[49]   See Jonathan Aitken, *John Newton: From Disgrace to Amazing Grace* (Wheaton: Crossway, 2007), 24.

of Godward contrition when Potiphar's wife attempts to seduce him. Genesis 39:12 says, "She caught him by his garment, saying, 'Lie with me.' But he left his garment in her hand and fled and got out of the house." Notice the decisive action of Joseph. He leaves no room for compromise. There is no time for talking. There is no time for negotiation. He simply ran as fast as he could. Joseph was a man of action. He was a man of contrition.

Confess Sin to Victims

Contrition not only involves confessing sin to God; it involves confessing our sin to those we have sinned against (Jas. 5:16). This kind of humble confession allows healing to take place in both the offender as well as the offended.

Keep Close with Other Believers Who Are Walking in the Light

Proverbs 13:20 says, "Whoever walks with the wise becomes wise, but the companion of fools will suffer harm." Thomas Watson understands the importance of staying in close contact with like-minded believers. He adds, "Nothing has a greater power and energy to effect holiness than the communion of the saints."[50] People who are serious about living a contrite life will link up with like-minded followers of Christ for mutual encouragement and accountability.

Realize the Tragic Effects of Unconfessed Sin

David learned the painful consequences of concealing his sin. Psalm 32:3-4 says, "For when I kept silent, my bones wasted away through my groaning all day long. For day and night your hand was heavy upon me; my strength was dried up

---

[50]   Thomas Watson, *A Body of Divinity* (Edinburgh: The Banner of Truth Trust, Reprinted 1992) 87.

as by the heat of summer" (Ps. 32:3-4). I remember a godly man in the church of my youth who referred to David's dilemma in this passage as a "bone ache." Since David concealed his sin, it affected his body and soul. It literally caused his bones to ache. We, along with King David, must realize the tragic effects of unconfessed sin.

Turn from Sin

A key mark of a contrite person is an ongoing hatred of sin. The person who hates his sin will quickly turn from his sin. J.C. Ryle remarks, "True repentance shows itself by producing in the heart a settled habit of deep HATRED of all sin."[51] Christ-followers committed to biblical contrition turn from sin by putting it to death each day. Therefore, we stand with the Puritans and make it our aim to mortify sin (Rom. 8:13). "The vigor, and power, and comfort of our spiritual life depends on the mortification of the deeds of the flesh," writes John Owen.[52] The Puritan pastor continues, "Be killing sin or sin will be killing you."[53] And Owen reminds us if left unchecked, "it will bring forth great, cursed, scandalous, soul-destroying sins."[54] So in pursuing God-centered contrition, we turn from our sin!

Refuse to Hide Sin

People who are authentically contrite refuse to hide their sin. Their aim is total transparency. Our responsibility is to be forthright. When we sin, we admit it. We understand our proclivity to conceal sin and mimic our father, Adam. So we refuse to hide sin. We bring it into the light to receive forgiveness and move forward on a path that honors God.

---

[51] J.C. Ryle, *Repentance* (Titus Books, 2012), Loc. 39ff.
[52] John Owen, *Of the Mortification of Sin in Believers - Volume 6* (Carlisle: Banner of Truth, 1967 reprint), 9.
[53] Ibid.
[54] Ibid, 12.

Refuse to Hurl Sin

The contrite are accountable. When they sin, they refuse to blame others for their sinful choices. Once again, they realize that all have a propensity to be like our father, Adam. Our tendency is to run from accountability and blame others for our depravity. When we refuse to hide our sin and hurl our sin, we model what authentic contrition truly looks like.

Hurling sin is something I have seen over and over as a pastor. When someone is confronted for their sin, they have a sinful tendency to hurl. Their tendency is to blame others for neglecting them, failing to hold them accountable, or failing in pastoral oversight. Perhaps these accusations have a kernel of truth. This withstanding, every person is still accountable to God for their sin. Therefore, in order to walk contritely before God, we refuse to hurl our sin.

Cling to the Cross of Christ

When we wander from the cross, we begin to compromise with sin. When we wander away from Calvary, we begin to doubt the promises of God. When we drift away from the cross, the lure of the world, the flesh, and the devil become more attractive. So we make it our aim to cling to the cross of Christ. Owen adds, "Hatred of sin as sin, not only as galling or disquieting, a sense of the love of Christ in the cross, lie at the bottom of all true spiritual mortification."[55] Calvin reminds us of the importance of such a pursuit: "For it is very certain that where God's grace reigns, there is readiness to obey it."[56]

This is the verdict: *God forgives sinners who confess their sin*. Scripture says, "As far as the east is from the west, so far does he remove our transgressions from us" (Ps. 103:12).

---

[55] Ibid, 41.
[56] *Institutes*, 2.3.11.

Isaiah 38:17 says, "Behold, it was for my welfare that I had great bitterness; but in love you have delivered my life from the pit of destruction, for you have cast all my sins behind your back." And Isaiah 43:25 encourages us, "I, I am he who blots out your transgressions for my own sake, and I will not remember your sins." Oh, that we would commit to being men and women of deep biblical contrition!

4
A TREMBLING MAN

We have seen that a person whose gaze is directed God-ward is humble. The person whose eyes are fixed on the Lord Jesus is contrite in spirit. The third defining mark of the Godward person is this: He or she trembles at God's Word.

John Calvin was a man who consistently trembled at God's Word. "Through his Word, God calls us to reverent love for him, a love that trembles with delight to do his will, and also trembles with fear, lest we fall short."[57] Calvin understood that trembling at God's Word was not optional. Rather, it was an essential component in a person who has his or her gaze fixated upon the living God.

As we come full circle, notice how these qualities depend upon one another. That is, they are intimately inter-related. Notice how contrition flows out of humility. And notice that a person trembles at God's Word as a result of humility and contrition.

For Calvin, trembling at God's Word was a daily habit. It became a part of the everyday fabric of his life. Listen carefully and you will detect the trembling in Calvin's demeanor:

When duly imbued with the knowledge of him, the whole aim of our lives will be to revere, fear, and worship his maj-

---

[57] Beeke & Smalley, *Reformed Systematic Theology: Revelation and God - Vol. 1*, 342.

esty, to enjoy a share in his blessings, to have recourse to him in every difficulty, to acknowledge, laud, and celebrate the magnificence of his works, to make him, as it were, the sole aim of all our actions ... Our conscience must, therefore, keep aloof from the most distant thought of revolt, if we would have our worship approved by the Lord. The glory of the Godhead must be maintained entire and incorrupt, not merely by external profession, but as under his eye, which penetrates the inmost recesses of his heart.[58]

TREMBLING AT WORMS

After Martin Luther made his stand at the *Diet of Worms* in 1521, he was whisked away by Fredrick the Wise and given sanctuary at the Wartburg castle. The Reformer lived under the alias *Junker George* as he holed away in seclusion for the better part of the year.

Luther used his time wisely during those days. The most productive thing he did was to translate the Greek New Testament into the language of the common man—the German tongue. Thanks to the first moveable type printing press, invented by Gutenberg in 1439, the German people could read the Word of God for the first time!

A few years ago, I had the pleasure of visiting Wartburg Castle in Germany. While the tour was fascinating, the room I wanted to see was scheduled at the end of our adventure. I wanted to stand in the room where Luther translated the Greek New Testament. As we neared the end of the tour, I ran ahead of our party so I could be alone in this room and soak in the history. I made my way into the room in isolation. It is a moment I will never forget!

---

[58]   *Institutes*, 2.8.16.

As I stood alone before Luther's desk, my eyes began to water and I was overcome with emotion and began to tremble. This is the room where the leader of the Protestant Reformation hid for the better part of a year. This is the room where Luther experienced intense spiritual warfare. This is the room where Luther labored over the text and produced a product that encouraged countless thousands of Christ-followers in Germany and beyond.

So it should come as no surprise that as I stood alone in that little room—I trembled. I trembled at the significance that stood before me. I trembled at the faithfulness of God who empowered a man of God to obey him. I was not trembling before a man or a movement. I was trembling before the Word of God.

THE POSTURE OF THE TREMBLING MAN

In a recent article, Al Mohler writes,

> *We dare to believe that God has spoken, that the Bible is his Word, that it bears divine authority and is without error. The secular mind cannot accept the audacious claim to believe that true morality flows from God's revelation, that God has spoken and established an order to his creation. The secular elites believe that anyone who holds to a biblical morality is a bigot and anyone who believes in divine revelation must be an idiot. In the view of the secular culture, that's where we stand.*[59]

Dr. Mohler provides the necessary context for understanding the trembling man. We tremble in the midst of a generation that views us as foolish. We tremble in the midst of a worldly system that views us with suspicion. We stand trembling amongst a sea of fools (Ps. 14:1).

---

[59] https://albertmohler.com/2019/02/07/knowing-stand-washington-post-columnist-says-anyone-holds-biblical-morality-bigot-calls-vp-pence-resign/

The Hebrew word for *tremble* means to "stand in awe and reverence of God's Word." Simply put, we tremble when we contrast ourselves with the majestic God of the universe in all his holiness. Calvin reminds us,

> *Men are never duly touched and impressed with a conviction of their insignificance, until they have contrasted themselves with the majesty of God. Frequent examples of this consternation occur both in the book of Judges and the prophetical writings ; so much so, that it was a common expression among the people of God, 'We shall die, for we have seen the Lord.'*[60]

How do we assume the posture of trembling? Would we, like ancient Israel respond with holy fear? There are at least five ways we can commit to trembling before the Word of God.

We Must Revere God's Word

God's Word is our highest authority. Listen to the reverence for God's Word in the book of Ezra:

> *Then all who trembled at the words of the God of Israel, because of the faithlessness of the returned exiles, gathered around me while I sat appalled until the evening sacrifice (Ezra 9:4).*

> *O my God, I am ashamed and blush to lift my face to you, my God, for our iniquities have risen higher than our heads, and our guilt has mounted up to the heavens (Ezra 9:6).*

John Calvin's reverence for the Word of God was unsurpassed and unwavering. He writes, "Moreover, the knowledge of God, which is set before us in the Scriptures, is designed for the same purpose as that which shines in creation, i.e., that we may

---

[60] *Institutes*, 1.1.3.

thereby learn to worship him with perfect integrity of heart and unfeigned obedience, and also to depend entirely on his goodness."[61] Again, as we have already noted, Calvin was a sinner who wrestled with sin and temptation as we all do. But what is especially striking is his desire to pursue integrity and be a man of "unfeigned obedience." This is the mark of a man who reveres the Word of God. This is the mark of a trembling man.

We Must Respect God's Word

In the church I pastor, we have a tradition of standing for the reading of God's Word before the sermon. This practice is a visible sign of respect for God's Word. It is a tangible way that we express the trembling which takes place in our hearts. Notice the posture of the people of God when Ezra opens the Word of God:

> *And Ezra opened the book in the sight of all the people, for he was above all the people, and as he opened it all the people stood. And Ezra blessed the LORD, the great God, and all the people answered, 'Amen, Amen,' lifting up their hands. And they bowed their heads and worshiped the LORD with their faces to the ground (Neh. 8:5-6).*

The person who trembles before the Word has a deep respect for the Word. Such a person listens attentively and responds obediently to Scripture. Instead of recoiling when the Word is declared, this person rejoices. Instead of arguing with Scripture, this person is filled with holy awe!

We Must Read God's Word

The trembling person reads the Word on a regular basis. He reads through books. He familiarizes himself with the flow of Redemptive history. Scripture admonishes us: "Hear the

---

[61]   Ibid., 1.10.2.

word of the Lord, you who tremble at his word ..." (Isa. 66:5a). Jeremiah writes, "Your words were found, and I ate them, and your words became to me a joy and the delight of my heart, for I am called by your name, O Lord, God of hosts" (Jer. 15:16). All those who tremble before the Word of God consume the Word of God as a daily habit. They count on God's Word to nourish and sustain them.

We Must Remember God's Word

Our call is to remember God's Word throughout the day. "You shall teach them to your children, talking of them when you are sitting in your house, and when you are walking by the way, and when you lie down, and when you rise" (Deut. 11:19). The word *remember* has more than a mere cognitive component where a given truth is internalized. To truly remember means that we must respond to the truth of God's Word.

Our call is to meditate on God's Word and to memorize God's Word. Scripture should be etched upon our hearts and minds. The psalmist writes, "I have stored up your word in my heart, that I might not sin against you" (Ps. 119:11).

We Must Rejoice in God's Word

God instructs us to rejoice in his Word as a matter of habit:

> *Blessed is the man who walks not in the counsel of the wicked, nor stands in the way of sinners, nor sits in the seat of scoffers; but his delight is in the law of the Lord, and on his law he meditates day and night (Ps. 1:1-2).*

> *I will meditate on your precepts and fix my eyes on your ways. I will delight in your statutes; I will not forget your word (Ps. 119:15-16).*

Your testimonies are my heritage forever, for they are the joy of my heart (Ps. 119:111).

This is the appropriate posture of the person who trembles before God's Word. While the surrounding culture totters, we tremble. And while the world assimilates anything and everything, we stand resolutely and choose to tremble before the Word of God.

THE PROTOTYPE OF TREMBLING

Israel

Israel is a prototype for what it means to tremble before God's Word. While we must admit that throughout her long history, Israel demonstrated periods of hard-heartedness and obstinate behavior, Scripture does indicate that Israel also trembled at God's Word.

In Nehemiah 8:1-12, we see remarkable evidence of this trembling. The people were *eager* to hear God's Word (v. 1). The people were *attentive* to God's Word (v. 3). They listened *reverently* to God's Word. And the people responded *joyfully* to God's Word: "*And all the people went their way to eat and drink and to send portions and to make great rejoicing, because they had understood the words that were declared to them*" (Neh. 8:12).

John Rogers

Consider another example of one who trembled before the Word of God. The smell of burning flesh hung in the air. The villagers turned their heads and gasped. Stray dogs fled. The man's wife wept bitterly. His children watched in disbelief. The stench was a vivid reminder of who sat upon the throne.

Mary Tudor ruled with ironclad authority. Her subjects were obligated to obey. Any dissenters would pay the ultimate price. The world would remember her as "Bloody Mary."

The day was February 4, 1555. The man roped to the pyre was well-known in the British village. He was a man of humble origins. A man with bold ambitions and simple obedience to match. A man who dared to challenge the carnal throne with two simple acts—*preaching* the Word of God and *printing* the *Matthews-Tyndale Bible*. His name was John Rogers—pastor, father, martyr. He was the first Christ-follower to pay the ultimate price of death during Mary's bloody reign of terror. He was the first of hundreds who would die at the hands of their blood-thirsty tyrant. John Rogers was a man who trembled at God's Word.

THE PAYOFF OF TREMBLING

There are many benefits of trembling before the Word of God.

It Leads to a Life of Blessedness

The psalmist unveils the benefits of the one who refuses to walk on an ungodly path: "Blessed is the man who walks not in the counsel of the wicked, nor stands in the way of sinners, nor sits in the seat of scoffers; but his delight is in the law of the LORD, and on his law he meditates day and night" (Ps. 1:1-2). The Hebrew word translated *blessed* means "happiness or highly favored."

Many evangelicals get extremely nervous about paying high regard for happiness. Some even suggest that God desires our holiness, not our happiness. But Psalm 1 stands opposed to this notion.

Randy Alcorn observes, "God made every source of pleasure, every reason for happiness. There has never been nor will there ever be any happiness in the universe that isn't from God."[62] Therefore, we do not fear happiness. Rather, we strive to be happy in God. "Above all things see to it that your souls are happy in the Lord … It is of supreme and paramount importance that you should seek above all things to have your souls truly happy in God himself."[63] And one of the best ways to be happy in the Lord is to tremble before his Word. This is a sure-fire way to a life of blessedness.

It Leads to a Life Which is Strengthened by the Truth of God's Word

When we tremble before God's Word, we place ourselves in a strategic place where we receive divine power. The apostle Paul prayed that the Ephesian believers would receive such a power:

> *For this reason I bow my knees before the Father, from whom every family in heaven and on earth is named, that according to the riches of his glory he may grant you to be strengthened with power through his Spirit in your inner being, so that Christ may dwell in your hearts through faith—that you, being rooted and grounded in love, may have strength to comprehend with all the saints what is the breadth and length and height and depth, and to know the love of Christ that surpasses knowledge, that you may be filled with all the fullness of God (Eph. 3:14–19).*

This power is available to every Christ-follower who trembles before God's Word.

It Leads to Freedom

Trembling before God's Word does not prohibit freedom; it produces it! Psalm 119:44-45 says, "I will always obey your

---

[62] Randy Alcorn, *Happiness* (Carol Stream: Tyndale House Publishers, 2015), 92.

[63] George Müller, Cited in Ibid, 100.

law, forever and ever. I will walk about in freedom, for I have sought out your precepts" (Psalm 119:44–45, NIV). The worldly system views the Word of God as "handcuffs" that hinder a life of pleasure. But nothing could be further from the truth. John Piper reminds us that "God is most glorified in us when we are most satisfied in him."[64] And the psalmist understands that living according to biblical precepts is the most liberating way to live. Trembling before the Word leads to freedom.

It Strengthens Convictions

Instead of strong convictions, many professing Christ-followers are an inch deep and a mile wide. We see compromise at every level—financial, ethical, moral, and sexual. It appears that nothing is out of bounds in our generation. Everything is accepted. Every lifestyle is tolerated. The postmodern milieu simply has no room for the transcendent, unchanging truths of God's Word.

Men and women who tremble before God's Word have convictions that are consistently strengthened. The psalmist, writing with fiery convictions says:

> *I hold back my feet from every evil way, in order to keep your word. I do not turn aside from your rules, for you have taught me. How sweet are your words to my taste, sweeter than honey to my mouth! Through your precepts I get understanding; therefore I hate every false way (Ps. 119:101-104).*

People with unswerving convictions are committed to truth and compelled to resist anything that is evil. The person of conviction heeds the counsel of Proverbs 1:15-16 - "My son do not walk in the way with them; hold back your foot from

---

[64] John Piper, *Desiring God: Meditations of a Christian Hedonist* (Sisters: Multnomah Books, 1996), 50.

their paths, for their feet run to evil, and they make haste to shed blood." The trembling Christian, then, is a person of unwavering conviction.

It Provides Direction

When we tremble before his Word, we not only walk on a secure path; we have the assurance that we're moving in the right direction. "Your word is a lamp to my feet and a light to my path" (Ps. 119:105). We're guided by the unfailing promises of the living God.

It Builds a Robust Christian Faith

The trembling person has a faith which is growing and robust. Such a person walks faithfully with Christ and lives for Christ. He or she is "rooted and built up in him and established in the faith ... abounding in thanksgiving" (Col. 2:6-7; c.f. Rom. 10:17).

THE PRINCIPLES OF TREMBLING

Finally, notice several principles that mark out the person who trembles at God's Word.

A Trembling Person Reads and Delights in God's Word

The psalmist says, "Blessed is the man who walks not in the counsel of the wicked, nor stands in the way of sinners, nor sits in the seat of scoffers; but his delight is in the law of the LORD, and on his law he meditates day and night" (Ps. 1:1-2). Over the years, I have routinely asked backslidden believers what the contributing factors were to their spiritual condition. The response is predictable: "I stopped reading the Word of God," they say. "I no longer cherished Scripture," they continue. A trembling person pays close attention to the mindset and habits of Jeremiah, who said, "Your words were found, and I ate them, and your words became to me a joy and the delight of my heart" (Jer. 15:16).

A Trembling Person Fears God

Listen to the wise admonition from Moses: "And now, Israel, what does the LORD your God require of you, but to fear the LORD your God, to walk in all his ways, to love him, to serve the LORD your God with all your heart and with all your soul" (Deut. 10:12). So fearing God involves a whole range of commitments. Such a person is passionately committed to the living God.

The first crucial step in knowing God is to fear him. "The fear of the LORD is the beginning of knowledge; fools despise wisdom and instruction," says Solomon (Prov. 1:7). So the trembling person one who fears God.

> *To know God as the Lord who dwells near his people is to fear him. Let us, therefore, humble ourselves with holy awe in the presence of the great 'I AM.' Let us consider his absolute independence from all limitations and his constant faithfulness to his covenant. Let us worship him with joy and trembling. He is the true God. In all this, let us trust him wholeheartedly as the only Redeemer.*[65]

Jerry Bridges argues that fearing God involves "reverential awe."[66] Thomas Watson says, "To fear God is to have such a holy awe of God upon our hearts, that we dare not sin." Beeke and Smalley offer this fitting warning: "Examine your heart for this grace of Word-inspired fear of the living God. If it is present, thank God and cherish it

---

[65]   Joel R. Beeke and Paul M. Smalley, *Reformed Systematic Theology: Revelation and God, Vol. 1*, 563-564.

[66]   Jerry Bridges, *The Joy of Fearing God* (Waterbrook Books, 2009), Loc. 300.

so that it grows. If it is absent, cry out for salvation, for you are lost."[67]

A Trembling Person Allows Scripture to Speak to Every Subject, Situation, and Discipline

Notice for instance how the Bible cuts through every academic discipline. The Bible, for instance, informs our approach to *biology*. The world says, "Life arose from the slimy algae by accident." The Bible says that God created every living creature.

The Bible informs our approach to *psychology*. The world says, "man is basically good." The Bible says that all people are sinners by nature and choice.

The Bible informs our approach to *counseling*. The world says, "Tell your counselee to believe in herself." The Bible says, "Him (Christ) we proclaim, warning everyone and teaching everyone with all wisdom, that we may present everyone mature in Christ" (Col. 1:28).

The Bible informs our approach to *science*. The world says, "The cosmos is a closed system. Miracles are impossible." The Bible says, "He is the radiance of the glory of God and the exact imprint of his nature, and he upholds the universe by the word of his power ..." (Hebrews 1:3a).

The Bible informs our approach to *education*. The world says, "Trust your knowledge; the answer is within." The Bible says, "The fear of the Lord is the beginning of knowledge" (Prov. 1:7). The world says, "Go to school, get smart, make a bunch of money, and die happy." The Bible says, "Therefore, as you received Christ Jesus the Lord, so walk in him, rooted and built up in him and established in the faith, just as you were taught abounding in thanksgiving" (Col. 2:7).

---

[67]   Beeke and Smalley, *Reformed Systematic Theology: Revelation and God - Vol. 1*, 343.

The Bible informs our approach to *law*. The world says, "Exploit people. Use them. Get your client to lie on the stand if it works in your best interest." The Bible says, "He has told you, O man, what is good; and what does the Lord require of you but to do justice, and to love kindness, and to walk humbly with your God?" (Micah 6:8).

The Bible informs our approach to *philosophy*. The world says, "Man is the measure." The Bible says, "See to it that no one takes you captive by philosophy and empty deceit, according to human tradition, according to the elemental spirits of the world, and not according to Christ" (Colossians 2:8).

And so, we tremble before the Word of God.

A Trembling Person Submits to the Lordship of God and Obeys His Word

John Frame helps us understand the importance of lordship: "God is the Lord of the covenant. Since God chose the name Lord (or Yahweh) for himself, since it is found thousands of times in Scripture, and since it is at the heart of the fundamental confession of faith of God's people (Deut. 6:4-5; Rom. 10:9), it would seem to be a promising starting point ... The central message of Scripture is that God is Lord."[68] A person who trembles at God's Word obeys God's Word. There are no qualifications. There are no clarifications. There are no escape hatches. God's Word is the highest authority in our lives—therefore we obey God's Word. The man who obeys God's Word trembles at God's Word.

A Trembling Person Refuses to Compromise the Bible

Some so-called "evangelical liberals" are quick to show allegiance to Scripture until it conflicts with one of their cher-

---

[68] John Frame, *The Doctrine of God* (Phillipsburg: Presbyterian and Reformed, 2002), 12.

ished beliefs or presuppositions. At the end of the day, they compromise, or completely discard any combination of the inerrancy, infallibility, sufficiency, and inspiration of Scripture. But these "evangelical liberals" must admit one thing: it is impossible to tremble at God's Word without affirming the authority, infallibility, sufficiency, and inspiration of sacred Scripture.

Kevin DeYoung's excellent book, *Taking God at His Word* summarizes the essence of our posture before God: "Submission to the Scriptures is submission to God. Rebellion against the Scriptures is rebellion against God."[69] DeYoung's heart for Scripture should be emulated by every person who seeks to live with a Godward gaze:

> *So let us not weaken in our commitment to our unbreakable Bible. Let us not wander from this divinely exhaled truth. Let us not waver in our delight and desire. God has spoken, and through that revelation he still speaks. Ultimately we can believe the Bible because we believe in the power and wisdom and goodness and truthfulness of the God whose authority and veracity cannot be separated from the Bible. We trust the Bible because it is God's Bible. And God being God, we have every reason to take him at his word.*[70]

And if we take him at his word, we tremble at his Word!

I want to challenge you to direct your gaze upward. As you commit yourself to being a person of humility, a person of contrition, and a person who trembles at God's Word, I am confident that you will truly live as a man or woman

---

69   Kevin DeYoung, *Taking God at His Word* (Wheaton: Crossway, 2014), 118.
70   Ibid, 123-124.

whose life is characterized by the Godward gaze. Your life will be set apart by God-centered resolve. The trajectory of your life will be heavenward. Your life will be distinguished by a passionate pursuit of the holy. May God use you for his purposes in the sphere of influence he has sovereignly placed you. May the gospel be the message that is proclaimed with your tongue. May the gospel be treasured in your heart and mind. And may the world be touched by the gospel message through your hands and feet. Then and only then will the world recognize that you are a Christ-follower on a special mission. Your gaze is sure to be Godward!

Epilogue

MORE CHRISTIANS LIKE CALVIN

There is a gaping chasm in the evangelical church. This chasm is a result of compromise and capitulation. It is the result of lazy thinking and lethargic living. This chasm has been produced by years of theological neglect, educational apathy, and lackadaisical leadership. The ungodly leaders that have emerged from the church have spawned a new generation of pragmatists which breeds a brand of progressive Christianity that helps no one.

We need more Christians like John Calvin—people whose gaze is Godward. We are in desperate need of leaders who are humble, contrite, and tremble before the Word of God. This is their holy pursuit. We need more Christian leaders like Calvin who trod faithfully on the path the leads to the Celestial City.

I Offer My Heart to God as a Sacrifice

In many respects, we are far removed from Calvin's day. In April, 1538, Calvin was driven out of Geneva when he refused to compromise his biblical convictions which concerned the administration of the Lord's Supper. Just over two years later, in October, 1540, Calvin was invited back to Geneva by his friend, William Farel. The prospect of returning to this place caused fear to rise within his soul: "There is no place under heaven that I am more afraid of—I would submit to death a hundred times rather than to that cross on which I had to die daily a thousand deaths."[71]

In a letter addressed to Peter Viret, Calvin refers to Geneva as "that place of torture."[72] Yet, this godly Reformer was determined to obey God and follow the prompting of the Holy Spirit. His response to Farel vividly shows the mixture of fear and reverence that consumed him: "If I had any choice I would rather do anything than give in to you in this matter, but since I remember that I no longer belong to myself, I offer my heart to God as a sacrifice."[73]

As Calvin began to pack his bags and make his way back to Geneva, he penned these words to Farel: "And for myself, I protest that I have no other desire than that, setting aside all consideration of me, they may look only to what is most for the glory of God and the advantage of the Church."[74] Calvin chose to boldly walk the path of obedience instead of treading on the convenient path of pragmatism. He writes, "Therefore I submit my will and my affections, subdued and held fast, to the obedience of God; and whenever I am at a loss for counsel of my own, I submit myself to those by whom I hope that the Lord himself will speak to me."[75]

This is exactly what we need in the church today. We need men and women of courage and conviction. We need people of character. We need people who say what they mean and mean what they say. We need nothing less than people who willingly and joyfully submit to the authority of God and his Word. We need more Christians like John Calvin.

---

[71]   John Calvin, Cited in *Letters of John Calvin*, xvii.
[72]   Ibid, 43.
[73]   John Calvin, Cited in Ibid, xviii.
[74]   Ibid, 45.
[75]   Ibid, 46.

In a stirring letter to William Farel dated October 24, 1538, Calvin points his dear friend, Godward: "But since the truth of the Lord remains firm and unshaken, let us stand resolutely upon the watch-tower even to the end, until the kingdom of Christ, which is now hidden and obscured, may shine forth."[76]

We need more Christians like Calvin because his desire was to be Christ-like. Scripture tells us of the single-minded resolve of the Lord Jesus Christ: "And being found in human form, he humbled himself by becoming obedient to the point of death, even death on a cross" (Phil. 2:8).

More Alive Than Ever Before

John Calvin breathed has last on May 27, 1564. He was buried in a common grave, a final act of humility, which was one of Calvin's final requests. The earthly life of the Genevan Reformer came to an end. But Calvin's death only signified the beginning of a new life with his Savior in his heavenly home. D.L. Moody reminds us that death is not the final chapter for a follower of Jesus Christ: "Soon you will read in the newspaper that I am dead. Don't believe it for a moment. I will be more alive than ever before."[77]

David W. Hall beautifully summarizes the life of the French reformer. He writes of Calvin: "A single man with heart aflame changed the world."[78] Calvin's influence began in Geneva as he faithfully exercised the gifts God bestowed upon him. He taught God's Word, preached God's Word, counseled with God's Word, and shepherded the flock with great care and patience. His pastoral ministry soon spread to

---

[76]   *Letters of John Calvin*, 29.

[77]   D.L. Moody, Cited in Randy Alcorn, *Heaven* (Wheaton: Tyndale House Publishers, 2004), 31.

[78]   David W. Hall, *The Legacy of John Calvin* (Phillipsburg: P&R Publishing, 2008), 38.

the corners of Europe and eventually made its way around the world. His ultimate aim had nothing to do with building his platform or attracting the eye of men. Rather, the aim of Calvin was to glorify the great God of the universe.

A Godward Gaze

John Calvin was a man whose gaze was Godward. His gaze was fixated upon his heavenly home. "Whom have I in heaven but you? And there is nothing on earth that I desire besides you" (Ps. 73:25). Calvin's life echoed the words of the psalmist as he gazed heavenward.

Calvin's gaze was fixated upon his Savior. "My flesh and my heart may fail, but God is the strength of my heart and my portion forever" (Ps. 73:26). For much of his adult life, Calvin battled with poor health. Yet, he continued to gaze upon his Savior. There was no wavering in this man. His faith in Jesus was solid until the end. This man fought the good fight. He finished the race. He kept the faith. And when he entered into his heavenly rest, his gaze was Godward.

Oh, that we would follow the lead of this godly man. May our lives be marked by humility, contrition, and trembling before God's Word. Then, and only then, will our gaze be Godward.

Soli Deo Gloria!

Made in the USA
Middletown, DE
22 May 2021